In the Community

At the Firehouse

By Julia Jaske

2 I see firefighters at the firehouse.

I see helmets at the firehouse.

4   I see masks at the firehouse.

I see dispatchers at the firehouse.

I see hoses at the firehouse.

I see water at the firehouse.

I see drivers at the firehouse.

I see ladders at the firehouse.

10 I see coats at the firehouse.

I see extinguishers at the firehouse.

I see dogs at the firehouse.

I see tanks at the firehouse.

Word List

firehouse hoses extinguishers
firefighters water dogs
helmets drivers tanks
masks ladders
dispatchers coats

72 Words

- I see firefighters at the firehouse.
- I see helmets at the firehouse.
- I see masks at the firehouse.
- I see dispatchers at the firehouse.
- I see hoses at the firehouse.
- I see water at the firehouse.
- I see drivers at the firehouse.
- I see ladders at the firehouse.
- I see coats at the firehouse.
- I see extinguishers at the firehouse.
- I see dogs at the firehouse.
- I see tanks at the firehouse.

Published in the United States of America by Cherry Lake Publishing Group
Ann Arbor, Michigan
www.cherrylakepublishing.com

Book Designer: Keri Riley

Photo Credits: cover: © BONDART PHOTOGRAPHY/Shutterstock; page 1: © BONDART PHOTOGRAPHY/Shutterstock; page 2: © VAKS-Stock Agency/Shutterstock; page 3: © VAKS-Stock Agency/Shutterstock; page 4: © Gorgev/Shutterstock; page 5: © Kzenon/Shutterstock; page 6: © Dusan Petkovic/Shutterstock; page 7: © VAKS-Stock Agency/Shutterstock; page 8: © chingyunsong/Shutterstock; page 9: © ChiccoDodiFC/Shutterstock; page 10: © Tyler Olson/Shutterstock; page 11: © Jens Molin/Shutterstock; page 12: © Sergey Mironov/Shutterstock; page 13: © Prath/Shutterstock; page 14: © Jeanne McRight/Shutterstock

Copyright © 2024 by Cherry Lake Publishing Group
All rights reserved. No part of this book may be reproduced or utilized
in any form or by any means without written permission from the publisher.

Note from publisher: Websites change regularly, and their future contents are outside of our control. Supervise children when conducting any recommended online searches for extended learning opportunities.

Cherry Blossom Press is an imprint of Cherry Lake Publishing Group.

Library of Congress Cataloging-in-Publication Data

Names: Jaske, Julia, author.
Title: At the firehouse / written by Julia Jaske.
Description: Ann Arbor, MI : Cherry Blossom Press, [2023] | Series: In the
  community | Audience: Grades K-1 | Summary: "At the Firehouse explores
  the sights and sounds of the firehouse. It covers people and objects
  found at the firehouse. Uses the Whole Language approach to literacy,
  combining sight words and repetition to build recognition and
  confidence. Simple text makes reading these books easy and fun. Bold,
  colorful photographs that align directly with the text help readers with
  comprehension"— Provided by publisher.
Identifiers: LCCN 2023003186 | ISBN 9781668927182 (paperback) | ISBN
  9781668929704 (ebook) | ISBN 9781668931189 (pdf)
Subjects: LCSH: Readers (Primary) | Fire stations—Juvenile literature. |
  LCGFT: Readers (Publications).
Classification: LCC PE1119.2 .J359 2023 | DDC 428.6/2—dc23/eng/20230221
LC record available at https://lccn.loc.gov/2023003186

Printed in the United States of America
Corporate Graphics